MAP 1

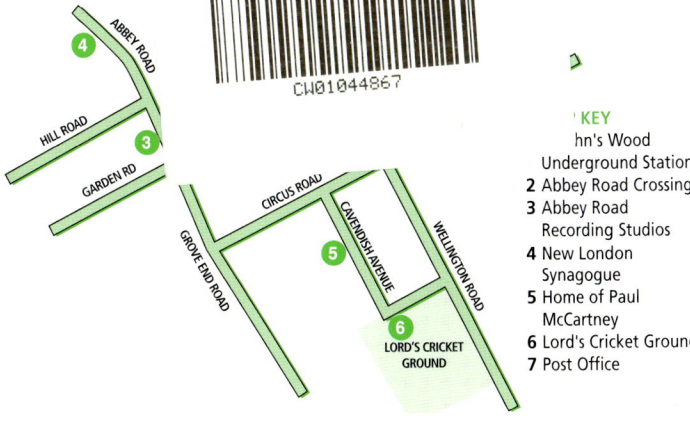

KEY
1 ~~St Joh~~n's Wood Underground Station
2 Abbey Road Crossing
3 Abbey Road Recording Studios
4 New London Synagogue
5 Home of Paul McCartney
6 Lord's Cricket Ground
7 Post Office

START OF WALK
STAGE 1: ABBEY ROAD RECORDING STUDIOS AND AREA

Directions: Start this walk at St John's Wood Underground Station ❶, which is on the Jubilee Line. Exit the Station. Cross over the road, which is directly ahead using the traffic lights. Continue directly ahead into Grove End Road. Keep walking on the right until you meet the junction at Abbey Road. Notice the smaller pedestrian crossing that crosses Abbey Road ❷ and not the larger crossing which are on your left and which cross Grove End Road.

Abbey Road Crossing: On 8th August 1969, the Beatles were photographed walking across this pedestrian crossing, during a ten-minute coffee break from a recording session at the nearby Abbey Road Recording Studios. The picture became the album cover for the Beatles' second to last album, called "Abbey Road". This famous road and the surrounding houses have not changed since 1969 and thousands of people visit here each year.

Directions: Cross the Abbey Road Crossing and turn right along Abbey Road. Almost at once on the left (at Nº 3) are the Abbey Road Studios ❸

Abbey Road Recording Studios: The Beatles first recorded here on 6th June 1962 and, over the past thirty years, the Studios have become a shrine to the Beatles, visited by fans from all over the world.

In April 1962, the then-unknown Beatles were playing in Hamburg when they received a telegram from Brian Epstein (see ❼) telling them that they had a recording session (and audition) with EMI at the Abbey Road Studios in June.

On 11th September 1962, the Beatles went on to record their first single, "Love Me Do", at the Studios. George Martin, their Producer, was not happy with the Beatles' drummer, Pete Best, whom he had seen at the audition in June, so he had a session drummer ready to play on the recording instead. Unknown to Martin, however, Best had been sacked and replaced by Ringo Starr. In September, when Ringo appeared, Martin still wanted his drummer to play. Although Ringo was finally allowed to play during the recording session, it is questionable whether Ringo's drumming actually appears on the A-side of the single. On the B-side, Ringo merely shakes the maracas!

The following year, the Beatles recorded their first album, "Please Please Me", at the Studios in just thirteen hours.

As the Beatles gained in popularity, this street was often full of young girls, who waited outside the Studios in the hope of seeing their idols. The Beatles would climb up the stairs to the rooftops to get fresh air, rather than venture out onto the street. The band often recorded at night, starting at 1.00 am. Hundreds of fans would camp outside all night with sandwiches and flasks.

The Abbey Road Studios have been described as the most important studios ever and are still used today by many of the world's top recording artists. Sting, Elton John, Pink Floyd, Cliff Richard, Oasis, the Police and the Jam have all used the Studios. Many musicians view working here (especially using Studio Two, in which the Beatles recorded) as a measure of how successful they have became. The members of Oasis, self-confessed Beatles fans, moved to live in this area just to feel close to their idols.

Directions: If you have time and were to continue to walk a further 2 km further along Abbey Road you will come to the New London Synagogue ❹

New London Synagogue: Here, on 17th October 1967, a memorial service was held for Brian Epstein. All the Beatles attended to pay their last respects to Epstein, who died in mysterious circumstances, after a drugs overdose.

Directions: Return back past the Abbey Road Studios and continue on the right hand side. Abbey Road now leads into Grove End Road. Cross over Grove End Road at the next set of traffic lights and turn into Circus Road, directly ahead. Continue along on the right hand side of Circus Road and take the second road on the right into Cavendish Avenue. On the right side of Cavendish Avenue is No 7 ❺ *the only house on the road not numbered.*

Nº 7 Cavendish Avenue: Since 1966 until Linda's unexpected death in 1998, this was Paul and Linda McCartney's London home. After Linda died, Paul and his family continued to live here when they were in London.

Paul bought the house in 1966 for a small fortune of £40,000; today, it is worth millions of pounds. Originally, Paul moved here with former girlfriend, Jane Asher. After coming home one evening unexpectedly, Jane allegedly found Paul with another woman; she packed her bags and left for good.

During the late 1960s, the house was very convenient, being so close to the Abbey Road Studios. The Beatles would often spend each night here before and after recording sessions. The house was also a regular meeting place for other famous artists who were staying in London; the list of guests includes Sting, Mick Jagger, Michael Jackson and Tina Turner.

In this house, Paul wrote many of his hit songs for the Beatles — including "Penny Lane", "Sergeant Pepper" and "Helter Skelter".

The house was constantly surrounded and sometimes invaded by fans, hence the big wooden gates and security. Paul once described how, during the Beatles' era, he hid in one of the bedrooms of the house opposite, and spied on the fans and the Press while they tried to spy on him. On another occasion, one warm summer night, Paul gave an impromptu performance of "Blackbird" to the fans waiting outside. The thrilled audience could hear Paul singing the ballad, while accompanying himself on an acoustic guitar, from the open window of the top floor music room.

If you are a cricket fan and you want to see the **Lord's Cricket Ground**, ❻ then continue to the end of Cavendish Avenue and turn left.

Directions: Go back the way you came along Cavendish Avenue. At the very end turn right into Circus Road and continue down here until you reach the junction with Wellington Road. Cross over Wellington Road and go to the Post Office ❼ *which is opposite to you and to the left.*

Post Office: It was from this Post Office, in April 1962, that Brian Epstein, after leaving a meeting at the Abbey Road Studios, sent a telegram to Hamburg to the Beatles, informing them of their audition at the Studios ❸

Directions: Exit the Post Office and go back to Wellington Road. Turn right down Wellington Road for approximately 300m and St John's Wood Underground Station is on the right hand side ❶

Directions: Take the Underground train only one stop to Baker Street (on the Jubilee Line). Please now follow Map 2 overleaf.

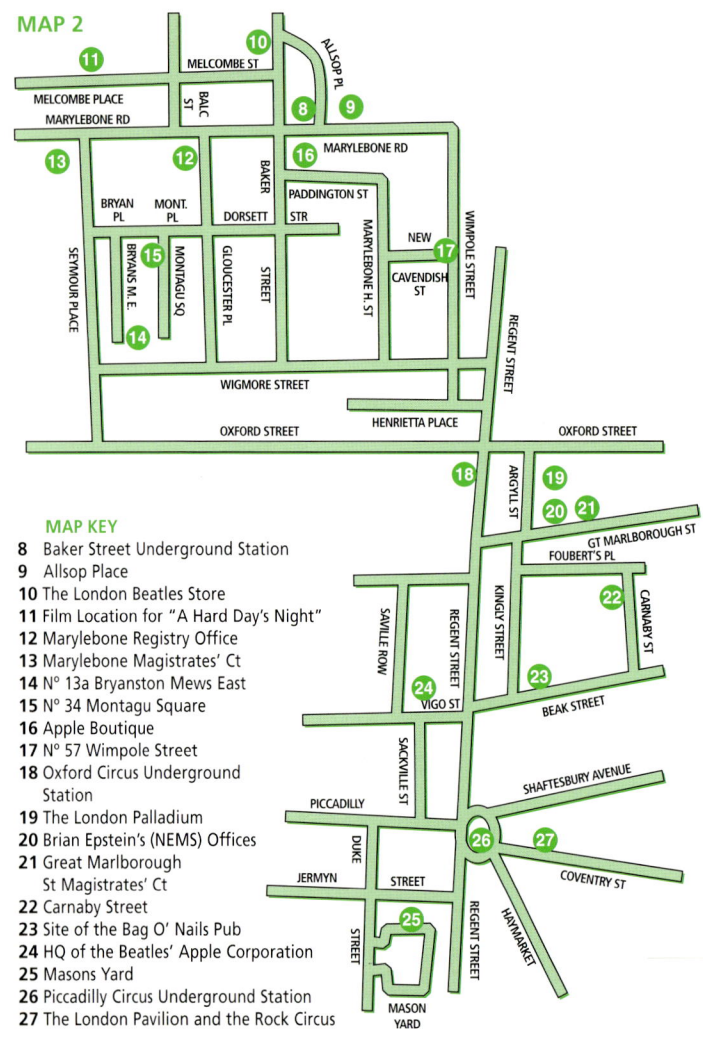

STAGE TWO: BAKER STREET TO PICCADILLY CIRCUS

Directions: Exit Baker Street Underground Station ❽. There are toilets inside this Station. Make sure you leave the Station at the Madame Tussaud's and Planetarium Exit. Turn left and continue to the corner of the first road on the left (just before the Planetarium) called Allsop Place ❾

Allsop Place: On this corner, on 11th September 1967, the Beatles' coach departed for a British tour, which was also made into the film "Magical Mystery Tour". The coach was late arriving, so Paul and the rest of the crew went into the nearby London Transport canteen for a cup of tea. Notice that a little further along, past the Planetarium is Madame Tussaud's Waxworks.

Directions: Continue into Allsop Place walking on the left hand side. Look out for the London Transport Canteen used by Paul and the crew on the left. Walk to the very end of Allsop Place until you arrive at Baker Street. Cross over Baker Street using the traffic lights directly ahead and when on the other side turn left outside the Volunteer Pub. Continue a little further and on your right at number 231 Baker Street you will arrive at the London Beatles Store ❿

The London Beatles Store: This shop is the first Beatles Store in London, and has a vast selection of Beatles goods – selling every kind of Beatles merchandise imaginable including postcards, tee shirts, posters and even cookie jars and musical globes. The shop also organises tours, events and runs the London Beatles Fanclub.

Directions: Exit the London Beatles Store and turn right. Continue and turn first right into Melcombe Street. Continue along on the left hand side and continue past Dorset Square, until you arrive at Marylebone Train Station ⓫, which is on the right hand side. Stop near the cobblestones that are outside the main entrance.

Marylebone Train Station: It was while filming "A Hard Day's Night" here in 1964 that, in one scene, John Lennon was required to run out of the Station and jump into a waiting taxi. In the film itself, on his way to the taxi, John rushes over the cobblestones, trips on one of them and falls over. This fall was not in the script, but was actually an accident. During filming, the whole Station was surrounded by screaming Beatles fans. These young girls were not extras brought in for the film, but actual fans who had discovered the film location and were all trying to get close to their idols.

Directions: Enter the Station by the main entrance. Turn left when inside and stop outside the "Food and Wine" Shop.

Food and Wine Shop: The entrance to the Shop was, until the 1980s, the main entrance to the station. In the film "A Hard Day's Night", there is a classic scene which involves the Beatles all standing in a line in front of a row of green telephone boxes. This scene was shot just inside the door to this Shop on the left wall. In another scene, the Beatles were filmed running into the Station from this entrance and running across the Station to Platform One.

Directions: Walk further along to the modern café on the left hand side which were called the Buffet Tea rooms in the 60's.

Buffet Tea Rooms: The building that houses the Buffet Tea Rooms has not changed at all since the film was shot. In the film, the Beatles are seen sitting at the small windows at the side of the Tea Room, drinking tea and looking out of the windows. Why not stop here, have a cup of tea and look out of the very same windows! (There are also toilets at this Station.)

Directions: Exit the Station through the main entrance and turn left down Melcombe Place. Keep to the right and turn down the second street on the right hand side, which is called Bolcombe Street. Walk to the end of Bolcombe street. Cross Marylebone Road at the traffic lights and turn left. The first large building on the right is the Marylebone Library and the second large building is Marylebone Registry Office **12**

Marylebone Registry Office (now Westminster Registry Office): At this Registry Office, there have been many famous marriages involving couples from the worlds of politics, pop and the theatre. One of the most famous marriage ceremonies was held on 12th March 1969 — when Paul McCartney married Linda Eastman. The other Beatles were not present, although George and Patti Harrison attended the wedding lunch at the Ritz afterwards. The crowds were so large that Paul and Linda were forced to enter the Registry Office from the rear alley, passing the rubbish bins on the way! After the ceremony, the couple left by the front entrance, standing on the large steps and waving to the crowd before being escorted away by a waiting car.

Also here in 1981, Ringo Starr married Barbara Bach and, more recently, in 1997, Liam Gallagher of Oasis married Patsy Kensit.

Directions: Go back past the Library, keep to the left hand side of the road and cross Upper Montagu Street. Continue nearly to the end of Marylebone Road, crossing several smaller roads. Stop just after crossing Seymour Place, as the raised building on the left hand side is Marylebone Magistrates' Court **13**

Marylebone Magistrates' Court: This famous Court closed in 1998 after 200 years of service. Here, in 1968, after being arrested at their flat ⑬, John and Yoko appeared before the Court for possession of cannabis. John pleaded guilty, was found guilty and fined £150, while Yoko was acquitted. Yoko was pregnant at the time, but she had a miscarriage shortly afterwards.

Sid Vicious (of the Sex Pistols) and his hapless girlfriend, Nancy Spungen, appeared here on drugs charges in 1978. Sid went on to greater things shortly afterwards: he allegedly killed Nancy with a hunting knife and then, having been charged with second degree murder, died from a drugs overdose.

Directions: Go back to the road you have just passed, which is at the side of the Court House and is called Seymour Place. Enter Seymour Place keeping on the left. Turn left at the fourth road on the left which is Bryanston Place. Enter and keep on the right hand side, walk past Bryanston Square and on the right you will come to N° 13a Bryanston Mews East ⑭

N° 13a Bryanston Mews East: In 1965, Mick Jagger tired of living with the other Rolling Stones in shared houses; so, he decided to move out and live alone for the very first time. He moved to this house and stayed here for almost one year. Please respect the privacy of the present-day occupants.

Directions: Continue along (Bryanston Square has now become Montagu Place) and only 20m further on the right is Montagu Square. Turn into the Square and immediately on the right is N° 34 Montagu Square ⑮
Please respect the privacy of the present occupants.

N° 34 Montagu Square: In 1965, Ringo Star bought this basement floor flat (second house along). He lived here alone for a while and then decided to rent it out. His first tenant was Paul McCartney, who used the flat as a mini recording studio and wrote several Beatles songs here.

Soon after Paul left the flat, Ringo found another tenant who had just arrived from America — the late Jimi Hendrix. Hendrix wrote many of his most famous songs while living here. It was soon clear that the new tenant was heavily involved with drugs and the Occult. Ringo evicted Hendrix four months later because Hendrix had painted every room in the flat black. The only light to be found in the whole flat was from dozens of candles.

After this, Ringo decided he would need to be more careful choosing his future tenants. So, in July 1968, he rented the flat to his old mate, John, and his new girlfriend, Yoko. John had just separated from his first wife (Cynthia) and this was the first home that he and Yoko shared together.

However, in October 1968, the police raided the flat in what turned out to be a high profile drugs bust. John was taken to Court ⑬ and fined. Years later, it was alleged that John had been tipped off about the drugs raid before it took place and so had ensured the flat was clean of all drugs. Also, the detective who had arranged the raid was himself prosecuted for allegedly planting drugs in people's homes and "fitting them up". It seems that John had known all along that he had been set up, but pleaded guilty to the charges to protect Yoko because she was a foreign national living in the UK and could have been deported if she had come under any investigation; also, she was pregnant.

The controversial album cover for John and Yoko's joint album called "Unfinished Music Nº 1 — Two Virgins" was taken in the bedroom of this flat. The picture showed the two standing completely naked in a full frontal pose. EMI records refused to distribute the record and a smaller independent label distributed it instead. John and Yoko were finally forced out of this flat after several of the neighbours complained about their strange activities! Ringo gave up being a landlord shortly afterwards and sold the flat!

Directions: Cross Montagu Square and continue further along Montagu Place. Cross over Gloucester Place at the traffic lights. Continue down Dorset Street until you arrive at the junction with Baker Street. Turn left and walk along Baker Street on the left until the first traffic lights. Cross over Baker Street and stop immediately on the corner of Baker Street and Paddington Street. On the opposite corner of Paddington Street at no 94 Baker Street (opposite the Bank) is the site of the famous Beatles' Apple Boutique ⑯

The Apple Boutique: In 1967, the Beatles were making a lot of money from their records. Their Accountants advised them that if they did not put money into a business, they would have to pay £3 million in tax. Consequently, the Beatles set up the Apple Corporation (or Apple Corp. as in "Apple Core"). The image of the apple used for the Company logo was suggested to Paul by a painting by Magritte, called "Le Jeu de Mourre" ("The Guessing Game"). Included amongst the different activities of the Apple Corporation were: Apple Records, Apple Music, Apple Films and a fashion outlet — the Apple Boutique.

The outside of the Apple Boutique was at first decorated with such bright coloured murals that the neighbouring shops took the Beatles to court. The Beatles lost the case and the murals were painted over in a sensible colour. The clothes shop became very popular, selling the top fashions of the day.

The Apple Corporation had its headquarters above the shop in the top flat. Sadly, after only seven months of trading, the shop was closed down due to bad management and financial chaos. The Apple Corp., however, flourished.

***Directions**: Turn right into Paddington Street, past the Paddington Street Gardens and walk to the very end. (Notice the British Telecom Tower towering above Marylebone High Street). Cross Marylebone High Street and turn right and continue along keeping on the left hand side. Continue until the second road on the left, which is called New Cavendish Road. Enter New Cavendish Road and keeping on the left hand side of the road, continue until you arrive at the third road on the left, which is Wimpole Street. Turn left into Wimpole Street and on the left you will arrive at Nº 57 Wimpole Street* **17**

Nº 57 Wimpole Street: This house belonged to the parents of the actress Jane Asher. Mr Asher was a doctor and Mrs Asher taught music at the Guildhall School of Music (George Martin was one of her pupils). Jane (aged only 17) met Paul at a Beatles concert at the Royal Albert Hall in April 1963. This was the start of their love affair. Only months after they first met, Paul moved into this house to live with Jane and her parents.

Paul lived here (in the rooms at the very top of the house) with the Asher family for three years and is reported as saying that these were some of the happiest times of his life. On the second floor at the front of the house was a music room. Paul and John often spent all night in this music room, with Paul at the piano and John playing an acoustic guitar. Together, they wrote many of famous Lennon and McCartney songs here.

Paul wrote "I Wanna Hold Your Hand" for Jane while living here; this became the Beatles' first US Nº1 hit. Another time, Paul woke up in the night with a tune in his head. He jumped out of bed and sat down at the piano beside the bed. He amazed himself by playing a complete song from start to end. At first, he thought it was someone else's song, which he had heard before. But, after he played it to John and others, it was clear that it was an original song and that Paul had, in fact, dreamt the tune. The song had no proper lyrics, so for over a year, its title was "Scrambled Eggs". Finally called "Yesterday", it was released as a single in the USA in 1965 and went to Nº 1. It was not released as a UK single, because the Beatles feared the release of a ballad would be bad for their image, and also that it would highlight one particular member of the band to the exclusion of the others. Yesterday has now been recorded by over 600 other artists.

In 1966, Paul bought a house in Cavendish Avenue **5** and he and Jane moved in there together.

Directions: Return down Wimpole Street to New Cavendish Street. Cross New Cavendish Street and continue to the very end of Wimpole Street, crossing Queen Anne Street and Wigmore Street on the way. Continue to the end to where you come to the junction with Henrietta Place. Cross the road and turn left down Henrietta Place and continue on the right hand side of the road, past Cavendish Square (on the left) until you reach Regent Street. Turn right down Regent Street and you will shortly arrive at Oxford Circus. To cross this busy road safely enter the Subway ⑱ to Oxford Circus Underground Station and exit the Subway at Exit 2 (Oxford Street East). When you exit the Underground Station, continue straight ahead along Oxford Street for only 20m or so. Turn into the first road on the right, which is called Argyll Street and a little further along on the left is the London Palladium ⑲

The London Palladium: This is the second largest theatre in London. The Beatles gave a live TV performance (for the variety programme "Sunday Night at the London Palladium") here in 1963; this was watched by over 15 million viewers. The reaction from fans was described by the Press as "Beatlemania". This was the first time the now well-known term was used.

Directions: A little further along, on the left, at Nºs 5–6 Argyll Street, are offices which once were Brian Epstein's NEMS Offices ⑳

Brian Epstein's NEMS Offices: Brian Epstein's company was called North End Music Stores (NEMS) Enterprises. The NEMS offices here became Brian Epstein's headquarters after the Beatles had become famous.

It is said to have been from these offices in 1966 that John Lennon described the Beatles to a London Evening Standard Journalist as being "more popular than Jesus". This offhand remark caused uproar, especially in the USA, where the Beatles were about to tour. During the 1966 tour, the Beatles were threatened by the Klu Klux Klan and their records were burned. This was to be the last tour by the Beatles, with their last live appearance in San Francisco in August.

Directions: Continue to the very end of the road to where Argyll Street meets Great Marlborough Street. Turn left up Great Marlborough Street. A little further, on your left, you will come to Nº 22 Great Marlborough Street, which is the Magistrates' Court ㉑

Magistrates' Court: Famous pop stars who have had to attend this Court (many on drug-related charges) include Brian Jones, Mick Jagger, Marianne Faithfull and even Johnny Rotten.

Directions: Cross Great Marlborough Street to the other side of the road (public toilets are here) and turn right back past the Liberty Department Store. Turn left into Kingly Street. Continue down Kingly Street keeping to the left. Turn second left into Foubert's Place and then first right, which will lead you into Carnaby Street ㉒

Carnaby Street: In the 1960s, when the Beatles lived in London, this Street represented to the world the image of "Swinging London". Mary Quant was based here, followed by many more designers. Fashion went into overdrive. Mini skirts, Afghan coats, love beads, joss sticks and drugs were everywhere. Later, in the 1980s, Neil Tennant, of the Pet Shop Boys worked here at Nºs 52-55 which were the offices of "Smash Hits" magazine. Boy George of Culture Club also worked in a shop in Carnaby Street before he was famous.

Directions: After exploring the area, continue to the very end of Carnaby Street. Turn right into Beak Street. Turn into the second road on the right, which is Kingly Street, and, on the right at no 9 was the Bag O' Nails Pub ㉓

Site of the Bag O' Nails Pub: Today, this building is a "Gentlemen's Club"; in 1967, it was a well known Jazz Club. On 15th May 1967, Paul was drinking here with friends, watching Georgie Fame playing. That evening, Paul was introduced to an American photographer named Linda Eastman. Romance grew, leading to one of the most successful music industry marriages, which lasted until Linda's tragic death from cancer in 1998.

Directions: Return to Beak Street. Turn right and continue to the very end to where it meets Regent Street. Cross Regent Street and turn left and walk down Regent Street keeping to the right. Turn third right into Vigo Street and then turn first right into Savile Row. (Savile Row is a world famous place to get made-to-measure suits.) Stop at Nº 3 on the right; this was the HQ of the Beatles' Apple Corporation ㉔

Headquarters of the Beatles' Apple Corporation: This building has had many uses over the years. During the early 1800s, Lord Nelson and his mistress, Lady Hamilton, lived here. In the 1950s, and up until the time the Beatles moved in it was a Gambling Den. In September 1968 the Beatles Corporation was formed and all the previous divisions moved here under one roof. Everyone who was anyone in the music business visited to meet the boys and to enjoy their generous hospitality. Derek Jones commented in a magazine "We've had many guests at Apple, friends. Can't remember any of them. Very stoned, you see. Affects the memory."

The Beatles built a recording studio in the basement. The main reason for the building's fame is that it was on its rooftop, on 30th January 1969, that the Beatles played together in front of an audience for the very last time. The "Let It Be" rooftop session lasted only 40 minutes. The last song the Beatles played, before the Bank opposite called the police, was "Get Back".

After Brian Epstein's death, the American accountant, Allen Klein, was brought in by John to sort out Apple's financial matters, which had got out of control. Although opposed by Paul, Klein became the Beatles' Business Manager and went on to dismiss many Apple staff. In June 1969, one of the newly vacant offices was taken over by John and Yoko for their own company, Bag Productions. Again, the rooftop was the venue for a unique event: this time a ceremony in which John legally changed his middle name from Winston to "Ono", becoming John Ono Lennon. The combination of John and Yoko's names now contained nine "o"s — nine was John's lucky number.

Directions: Leave Savile Row the way you entered it and turn left into Vigo Street. Continue and turn first right down Sackville Street. Continue to the end of the Street to where it meets with Piccadilly. Turn left and cross Piccadilly at the traffic lights. Then, when on the other side of the road, turn right. Turn into the first road on the left, which is Duke Street, but labelled as: Duke Street St James's. Continue along on the left and cross Jermyn Street and continue. Turn into the second road on the left (just after N° 17 Duke Street) which is called Mason's Yard. Enter Mason's Yard ㉕ and stop at N° 6, which is on the left hand side of the Yard. In this building, in the 1960s, was a famous art gallery called the Indica Gallery.

The Indica Gallery: It was inside this small gallery, in 1966, that John and Yoko first met. Yoko had a conceptual artwork exhibition here and had invited celebrity guests to the opening in the hope of getting some financial backing. When John arrived, Yoko gave him a scrap of paper with the word "Breathe" scribbled onto it. Later on, John noticed a piece of Yoko's artwork on the ceiling; using a ladder, he climbed up to have a closer look. He asked Yoko if he could bang a nail into the picture (called "Painting to Hammer a Nail In"). Yoko replied yes, but it would cost him five shillings. John then asked if he could hammer an imaginary nail into the picture instead.

Although, at that time, John was married to Cynthia and Yoko was married to Tony Cox, this was the start of an intense love affair that lasted virtually unbroken up until the time of John's tragic murder on 9th December 1980.

Directions: A little further along in the corner of the Yard is N°13.